POSTCARDS FROM

Aunt Bee's

MAYBERRY COOKBOOK

Ken Beck and Jim Clark
Recipes edited by Julia M. Pitkin

Rutledge Hill Press
Nashville, Tennessee

D0191073

Published in Nashville, Tennessee by Rutledge Hill Press, Inc. 211 Seventh Avenue North, Nashville, Tennesseee 37219. Distributed in Canada by H. B. Fenn and Company Ltd., Mississauga, Ontario.

Design by Harriette Bateman/Robert Schwalb

Printed in Mexico

1 2 3 4 5 6 7 8 9 – 95 94 93

Introduction

Welcome to this snack pack of recipes and pictures straight from the heart of Mayberry.

Now you can share special greetings from Mayberry with your family and friends. After all, Mayberry is known far and wide as the friendly town, the peaceful place that everybody would like to call home.

Postcards from Aunt Bee's Mayberry Cookbook is filled with Mayberry's down-home warmth and friendliness. These recipe postcards include photographs of all of your favorite characters from "The Andy Griffith Show," along with thirty of the most mouth-watering recipes from *Aunt Bee's Mayberry Cookbook*.

With this postcard book, you can sample some of the cookbook's very best dishes and desserts that bring out the full flavor of Mayberry. Of course, Aunt Bee would want you to enjoy all of the recipes yourself—especially the pickles.

But we know she'd be even more pleased for you to share these postcards with others when you have occasion to write them.

Many of the recipes on these postcards come from the kitchens of the cast and writers of "The Andy Griffith Show." The recipes they selected are ones they felt would be most fitting for their Mayberry characters, plus ones that are just plain delicious.

Other recipes on the postcards are scrumptious fare from some of the finest cooks in the land. If you like the variety of treats on these postcards, you'll discover a Mayberry feast of recipes waiting to twang your taste buds in the cookbook itself.

As much as the recipes, the photographs are sure to stir happy memories and bring a big smile to the face of anyone who receives one of the cards.

So with pen and fork in hand, have fun sharing these helpings of Mayberry food for thought and tummy. And remember, as Andy always says, "Eatin' speaks louder than words." Yum!

—*Ken Beck and Jim Clark*

Ernest T. Bass Rock Bars

½ cup butter
¼ cup plus 2 tablespoons sugar
¼ cup plus 2 tablespoons brown sugar
1 teaspoon vanilla extract
1 egg
1 cup all-purpose flour
½ teaspoon baking soda
½ teaspoon salt
½ cup coarsely chopped walnuts
1 6-ounce package semisweet chocolate chips

Grease and flour a 9 x 13-inch pan. In a large bowl cream the butter, sugar, brown sugar, and vanilla. Beat in the egg. In a separate bowl sift together the flour, soda, and salt. Blend the dry ingredients into the creamed mixture, and add the nuts. Spread the batter into the prepared pan, and sprinkle chocolate chips over the top. Bake in a 375° oven for 1 minute, remove, and score with a knife to create a marbled effect. Return to the oven and bake for 13 to 16 minutes or until golden brown.
   Serves 12.

HERE COMES THE BRIDE?
Ernest T. Bass is tricked into thinking Barney is Charlene Darling in "Mountain Wedding."

Recipe from page 216 in *Aunt Bee's Mayberry Cookbook*
Rutledge Hill Press, Nashville, Tennessee

Goober's Radiator Flush Punch

2 cups prepared tea
Juice of 2 oranges
1 12-ounce can orange soda
Juice of 1 lemon
1 cup ginger ale
Orange and lemon slices

In a pitcher combine all of the ingredients. Serve over ice.

This is best when served with comic books.

Makes 5 cups.

GOOBER SAYS HEY!
When you've got something to say, Goober's all ears.

Recipe from page 30 in *Aunt Bee's Mayberry Cookbook*
Rutledge Hill Press, Nashville, Tennessee

Miss Crump's Gold Star Gazpacho

2 large ripe tomatoes
1 large sweet green pepper
1 clove garlic
Salt to taste
½ cup chopped mixed herbs (chives, parsley,
    basil, chervil, tarragon)
½ cup olive oil
3 tablespoons lemon or lime juice
3 cups chilled water
1 sweet Spanish onion, peeled and diced
1 cup peeled, seeded, and diced cucumber
1½ teaspoons salt or to taste
½ teaspoon paprika

Peel and seed the tomatoes. Seed and remove the
membrane from the pepper. Cube, chop, or dice
the tomatoes, pepper, and garlic. In a large bowl
combine the chopped tomatoes, pepper, and garlic, and add salt. Add the herbs. Gradually stir in
the oil, lemon juice, and water. Add the remaining
ingredients. Chill for at least 4 hours. Cold and
crunchy!
    Serves 8.
—*Aneta Corsaut (Helen Crump)*

LOVE NOTES

Andy's not the only one who has a crush on Helen.

Recipe from page 33 in *Aunt Bee's Mayberry Cookbook*
Rutledge Hill Press, Nashville, Tennessee

Mr. McBeevee's Make-ahead Breakfast

1 pound hot sausage
6 slices bread, cubed
1 cup grated cheese
6 eggs
2 cups milk
1 teaspoon salt
1 teaspoon mustard

In a skillet crumble and cook the sausage until browned. Drain. Grease a 9 x 13-inch pyrex pan and line the bottom with cubed bread. Top with sausage and cheese. In a bowl combine the eggs, milk, and seasonings. Beat well and pour over the layers in the pan. Cover and refrigerate overnight.

Bake in a 350° oven for 30 minutes. Cut into squares and serve. Serves 6 to 8.

HARD TO BEAT
Aunt Bee's breakfast is everything it's cracked up to be.

Recipe from page 61 in *Aunt Bee's Mayberry Cookbook*
Rutledge Hill Press, Nashville, Tennessee

Nora Belle's Cheese Soufflé

4 tablespoons butter
2 tablespoons flour
½ teaspoon salt
Dash cayenne pepper
1 cup scalded milk
½ cup or more grated
    sharp cheddar
    cheese
4 egg yolks, beaten
4 egg whites, beaten
    stiff

Butter a 1-quart soufflé dish. In a saucepan or double boiler over simmering water melt the butter. Add the flour and blend well. Add the salt and cayenne. Gradually add the scalded milk. Cook, stirring constantly, until thick and smooth. Add the cheese and stir until the cheese is melted and the sauce is smooth. Remove from the heat and add the egg yolks. Blend well and allow to cool. Fold in the stiffly beaten egg whites. Turn the mixture into the prepared soufflé dish, and set in a pan of hot water. Bake in a 325° oven for 45 minutes to 1 hour, depending on how moist you wish the soufflé to be.

Serves 3 to 4.

READALL ABOUT IT
Andy, Opie, and Aunt Bee share all the news from Mayberry.

Recipe from page 67 in *Aunt Bee's Mayberry Cookbook*
Rutledge Hill Press, Nashville, Tennessee

Gomer's Banana Bread Pyle

1 cup butter or oil
2 cups sugar
4 eggs, beaten well
6 to 7 bananas, mashed
2½ cups sifted all-purpose flour
1 teaspoon salt
2 teaspoons baking soda
½ cup chopped macadamia nuts

Grease 2 large loaf pans or 5 small ones.
Cream the butter with the sugar. Add the
eggs and beat well. Add the mashed
bananas, stirring to blend. In a separate
bowl sift together the dry ingredients. Fold
the dry ingredients into the batter, mixing
well. Add the macadamia nuts. Pour the
batter into the pans. Bake in a 350° oven for
50 to 60 minutes, or until done.

For muffins, fill 12 muffin cups ¾ full
and bake in a 350° oven for 35 to 45
minutes.

Makes 2 large loaves, 5 small loaves,
or 12 large muffins.
—*Jim Nabors (Gomer Pyle)*

SHAZAM!

Barney and Gomer are always full of surprises.

Recipe from page 71 in *Aunt Bee's Mayberry Cookbook*
Rutledge Hill Press, Nashville, Tennessee

Carolina Corn Pone

1 cup cornmeal (not self-rising)
1 teaspoon salt
1 cup boiling water (more as needed)
2 tablespoons bacon drippings or oil

In a bowl combine the cornmeal and salt. Add the boiling water slowly, stirring to remove the lumps. Add enough water to make a medium batter. Using a cookie sheet with sides, heat it and the bacon drippings or oil. Coat the pan with the hot oil. Pour the hot drippings into the cornmeal mixture. Stir well. Using a large mixing spoon, drop the batter onto the cookie sheet by the spoonful. Pat a little with the back of the spoon. Bake in a 400° oven for about 25 minutes. The corn pone should be crusty on the bottom and soft in the center.

Serves 4 to 6.

SKILLET SKILLS

Andy fries up a little breakfast on the shore of Myers' Lake.

Recipe from page 83 in *Aunt Bee's Mayberry Cookbook*
Rutledge Hill Press, Nashville, Tennessee

Thelma Lou's Neighborly Popovers

3 eggs
1 cup milk
1 cup sifted all-purpose flour
½ teaspoon salt
1 tablespoon butter or margarine,
melted

Grease ten 5-ounce ovenproof custard
cups. In a large bowl beat together all
of the ingredients with an electric mixer
or rotary beater. Pour the batter into
the cups, filling them about ⅓ full. Bake
in a 400° oven for about 35 minutes,
until the popovers are firm, crusty, and
golden.

Makes 10 popovers.
—*Betty Lynn (Thelma Lou)*

"YOU'RE THE CAT'S!"

Barney thinks there's nobody sweeter in Mayberry than Thelma Lou.

Recipe from page 87 in *Aunt Bee's Mayberry Cookbook*
Rutledge Hill Press, Nashville, Tennessee

Barney's Salt and Pepper Steak

1½ pounds sirloin steak
½ cup oil
1 onion, chopped
1 green pepper, chopped
½ teaspoon salt
¼ teaspoon pepper
3 tablespoons all-purpose flour
1 cup water
3 tablespoons soy sauce
Cooked rice

Cut the steak into very thin slices. In a skillet with a lid heat the oil and add the steak slices. Cook uncovered until browned. Pour out some of the oil and add the remaining ingredients except the rice. Cover and cook for 30 to 35 minutes, until the juice has thickened. Serve over rice.

Serves 4 to 6.

PARTY TIME

Andy and Barney are well-suited for their Mayberry
Union High School class reunion.

Recipe from page 99 in *Aunt Bee's Mayberry Cookbook*
Rutledge Hill Press, Nashville, Tennessee

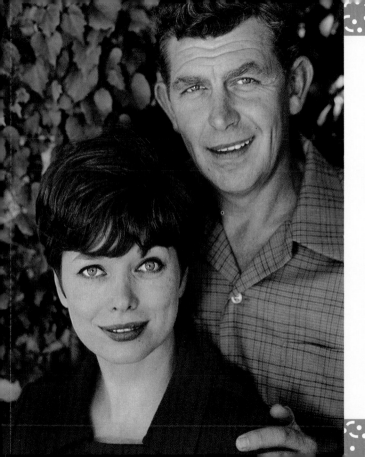

Orange Chicken Helen

4 chicken breasts, boned and skinned
Butter
Salt
Orange juice
Tabasco sauce
Orange sections
Currants
Raisins
Diced walnuts (optional)
Rice pilaf

Flatten the chicken breasts slightly. In a skillet heat a small amount of butter and cook the chicken breasts for about 5 minutes on each side. Salt lightly. Add orange juice to cover, and simmer for a few minutes. Add Tabasco sauce to taste, orange sections, currants, raisins, and walnuts as desired. Cover and simmer for about 25 minutes, until the chicken is tender. Check, and add more orange juice if needed.

Serve with rice pilaf.
Serves 4.
Aneta Corsaut (Helen Crump)

MAYBERRY LOVE STORY

Andy and Helen go down in history as one of Mayberry's most memorable romances.

Recipe from page 113 in *Aunt Bee's Mayberry Cookbook*
Rutledge Hill Press, Nashville, Tennessee

Pipe Down Pork Chop Casserole

4 or 5 potatoes
4 or 5 pork chops
1 10½-ounce can cheddar cheese
** soup**
1 10½-ounce can French onion soup

Slice the potatoes into a 9 x 11-inch casserole dish. Arrange the pork chops over the potatoes. Combine the soups and pour over the pork chops and potatoes. Cover with foil. Bake in a 350° oven for 1 hour.

Serves 4.

BUM STEER

Barney gives Otis an earful for horsing around.

Recipe from page 128 in *Aunt Bee's Mayberry Cookbook*
Rutledge Hill Press, Nashville, Tennessee

Pan-fried Flounder Floyd

½ cup oil
½ cup cornmeal
2 teaspoons salt
¼ teaspoon pepper
¼ teaspoon garlic powder
2 pounds flounder fillets

In a skillet heat the oil over medium heat. In a shallow dish combine the cornmeal, salt, pepper, and garlic powder. Roll the fish in the cornmeal mixture and drop in the hot oil. Fry for 3 to 5 minutes, until browned. Turn and brown on the other side.

Serves 4 to 6.

MAYBERRY CLIPPER

Floyd the Barber keeps cutting up while waiting for his dream of a two-chair shop to come true.

Recipe from page 139 in *Aunt Bee's Mayberry Cookbook*
Rutledge Hill Press, Nashville, Tennessee

Hollister Hoppin' John

1 pound bulk pork sausage, broken into
    small chunks
4 cups water
1 large onion, roughly minced
2 cups purple hull or crowder peas
Salt
Hot sauce
Steamed rice
Cornbread

In a Dutch oven lightly brown the
sausage. Drain. Do not overbrown the
sausage, as that will render all of the fat
and most of the flavor. Add the water,
onion, and peas. Bring to a boil, cover,
and simmer for 30 to 40 minutes. Remove
the lid and simmer, stirring occasionally,
until the pot liquor thickens. Add salt and
hot sauce to taste. Serve over steamed
rice with cornbread.
    Serves 4 to 6.
Jack Prince (Rafe Hollister)

STILL LIFE
Rafe Hollister's singing always shines in Mayberry.

Recipe from page 150 in *Aunt Bee's Mayberry Cookbook*
Rutledge Hill Press, Nashville, Tennessee

Baked Goober Beanies

2 1-pound cans pork and beans,
partially drained
¾ cup brown sugar
2 teaspoons dry mustard
5 slices bacon, chopped
½ cup catsup

Empty one can of beans into a 1½-quart
casserole dish. Combine the brown
sugar and mustard, and sprinkle half
over the beans. Top with the other can
of beans and sprinkle with remaining
brown sugar, chopped bacon, and
catsup. Bake uncovered in a 325° oven
for 2½ hours.

Serves 4 to 6.

MAYBERRY'S TOP DOGS
Goober finds that it's hard to teach an old dog new tricks.

Recipe from page 150 in *Aunt Bee's Mayberry Cookbook*
Rutledge Hill Press, Nashville, Tennessee

Tex Foley's Cowboy Soup

1 pound ground beef
½ cup chopped onion
1 16-ounce can mixed vegetables
1 10-ounce can Rotel tomatoes
1 13-ounce can Spanish rice
1 14½-ounce can stewed tomatoes
1 17-ounce can cream-style corn

In a large stock pot brown the ground beef and onion. Add the remaining ingredients, cover, and simmer for about 1 hour.

Serves 6.

OH MY DARLINGS
Andy has his hands full whenever the Darlings come to town.

Recipe from page 34 in *Aunt Bee's Mayberry Cookbook*
Rutledge Hill Press, Nashville, Tennessee

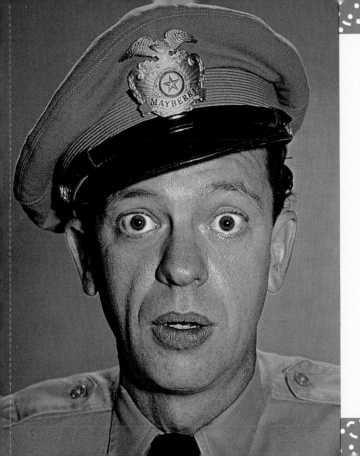

Mr. Schwump's Sweet Potato Soufflé

3 cups cooked, mashed sweet potatoes
½ cup orange juice
½ cup milk
1 teaspoon vanilla extract
½ cup sugar
½ teaspoon salt
6 tablespoons butter, melted
Cinnamon
½ cup brown sugar
⅓ cup all-purpose flour
1 cup chopped pecans
Marshmallows

Grease a baking dish. In a mixing bowl combine the sweet potatoes, orange juice, milk, vanilla, sugar, salt, 3 tablespoons of melted butter, and cinnamon. Beat until fluffy, and pour into the prepared baking dish. Melt the remaining butter and add the brown sugar, flour, and pecans. Sprinkle the mixture over the potatoes. Bake in a 350° oven for 35 minutes. Top with marshmallows and bake until browned.

Serves 6.

NIP IT IN THE BUD!

No reason to panic. With Barney on patrol, everything's A-O.K. on the streets of Mayberry.

Recipe from page 167 in *Aunt Bee's Mayberry Cookbook*
Rutledge Hill Press, Nashville, Tennessee

Ellie's Confetti Vegetables

1 cup mashed cooked carrots
1 cup frozen chopped broccoli, thawed
1 10-ounce package frozen whole kernel corn,
    thawed
1 cup milk
1 cup cracker crumbs
½ cup shredded sharp cheddar cheese
¼ cup minced onion
⅓ cup melted butter
Salt and black pepper to taste
⅛ teaspoon cayenne pepper
4 eggs

Butter a round 2-quart glass baking dish. In a
large mixing bowl combine the carrots, broccoli,
corn, milk, cracker crumbs, cheese, onion, and
butter. Season with salt, pepper, and cayenne.

    In a separate bowl beat the eggs until frothy.
Blend lightly into the carrot mixture. Pour the
mixture into the prepared dish. Bake in a 350°
oven for 40 to 45 minutes or until a knife inserted
near the center comes out clean.

    Serve hot or at room temperature. This
reheats very well.

    Serves 6 to 8.

—*Elinor Donahue (Ellie Walker)*

FRIENDLY PHARMACIST

With her patented smile, Ellie Walker always has the right prescription for Mayberry.

Recipe from page 168 in *Aunt Bee's Mayberry Cookbook*
Rutledge Hill Press, Nashville, Tennessee

Opie's Carrot-top Cake

1½ to 2 cups sugar
1½ cups oil
4 eggs, beaten
2 cups self-rising flour
2 teaspoons cinnamon
1 teaspoon vanilla extract
2 to 3 cups grated carrots
½ cup chopped nuts
¼ cup margarine
1 8-ounce package cream cheese
1 1-pound box confectioners' sugar
1 teaspoon vanilla extract
Milk, if needed

Grease and flour 3 cake pans. In a large bowl
combine the sugar, oil, eggs, flour, cinnamon,
1 teaspoon of vanilla, carrots, and nuts in the
order given. Pour into the prepared pans. Bake
in a 300° oven for about 30 minutes.

Cream together the remaining ingredients,
adding milk if necessary to make the icing
spreadable. Spread on the cooled cake.

Serves 10 to 12.

KIDDING AROUND

Andy (to Opie at picnic): "If you eat any more, you'll swell up so tight, your freckles will fall off."

Recipe from page 174 in *Aunt Bee's Mayberry Cookbook*
Rutledge Hill Press, Nashville, Tennessee

Juanita's Ginger Cookies

¾ cup shortening
1 cup sugar
4 tablespoons molasses
¼ teaspoon salt
1 egg
2 cups all-purpose flour
3 teaspoons baking soda
1 teaspoon cinnamon
1 teaspoon ginger
½ teaspoon cloves

Grease a cookie sheet. In a large bowl cream together the shortening and sugar. Add the molasses, salt, and egg, and blend well. In a separate bowl sift together the dry ingredients. Blend into the creamed mixture. Shape the dough into small balls and roll in granulated sugar. Place on a greased cookie sheet. Bake in a 350° oven for 10 to 12 minutes.

Makes about 6 dozen cookies.

FOUR-PART HARMONY

Double-dating is twice as much fun for Andy and Helen and Barney and Thelma Lou.

Recipe from page 213 in *Aunt Bee's Mayberry Cookbook*
Rutledge Hill Press, Nashville, Tennessee

Harriet's Caramel Nut Pound Cake

1 cup butter
¼ cup shortening
1 1-pound box brown sugar
1 cup sugar
5 eggs
3 cups cake flour
½ teaspoon salt
1 teaspoon baking powder
1 tablespoon vanilla extract
1 cup milk
1 cup finely chopped black walnuts

Grease and flour a 10-inch tube pan. In a large bowl cream the butter and shortening. Add the brown sugar and sugar. Add the eggs one at a time, beating until creamy. Sift together the flour, salt, and baking powder, and add alternately with the milk and vanilla until blended well. Fold in the nuts. Pour into the prepared pan. Bake in a 325° oven for 1 hour, or until a cake tester inserted near the center comes out clean.

Serves 8.

GOOBER SAYS HALT?

You need to know the password to be admitted to Mayberry's
Regal Order of the Golden Door to Good Fellowship.

Recipe from page 176 in *Aunt Bee's Mayberry Cookbook*
Rutledge Hill Press, Nashville, Tennessee

Aunt Bee's Apple Pie

½ cup butter or margarine
4 ounces cream cheese
2 cups all-purpose flour
2½ cups sliced apples
1 cup sugar
⅓ cup orange juice
2 tablespoons honey
½ teaspoon cinnamon
1 tablespoon all-purpose flour
½ cup butter or margarine

In a large bowl combine ½ cup of butter and the cream cheese, and let come to room temperature. Add 2 cups of flour, and blend well. Chill. Roll out half of the dough and place in a 9-inch pie plate. Reserve the remaining dough for the top crust.

In a saucepan combine the remaining ingredients and bring to a boil. Pour the mixture into the crust. Roll out the remaining crust and place over the filling. Cut slits in the top crust to allow steam to escape. Bake in a 350° oven for 45 minutes.

Serves 6 to 8.

BEE SWEET

Nothing says Mayberry better than Aunt Bee's
homemade apple pie. Mmm, Mmm!

Recipe from page 185 in *Aunt Bee's Mayberry Cookbook*
Rutledge Hill Press, Nashville, Tennessee

Opie and Leon's Favorite Buttermilk Pie

2 cups sugar
1 teaspoon cinnamon
1 teaspoon nutmeg
1 teaspoon vanilla extract
2 tablespoons cornstarch
½ cup melted butter
3 large eggs
1 cup buttermilk
1 9-inch pie shell

In a large bowl combine the sugar, cinnamon, nutmeg, vanilla, cornstarch, butter, and eggs. Beat with an electric mixer on low speed until well blended and uniform. Add the buttermilk and mix well. Pour into the pie shell. Bake in a 350° oven for 40 minutes, or until set and brown on the top.

Serves 6 to 8.

—*Mrs. Rance Howard (Ron and Clint's mom)*

SUBURBAN COWBOYS

This recipe was the favorite dessert of brothers Ron and Clint Howard (Opie and Leon) during their years on "The Andy Griffith Show."

Recipe from page 188 in *Aunt Bee's Mayberry Cookbook*
Rutledge Hill Press, Nashville, Tennessee

Campbell Cranberry Pie

2¾ cups cranberries
2 cups sugar
2 teaspoons cornstarch
4 tablespoons all-purpose flour
½ cup brandy or orange juice
Pastry for 1 8-inch two-crust pie

In a large bowl combine the cranberries, sugar, cornstarch, flour, and brandy. Turn the mixture into the pie crust and top with the remaining pastry. Bake in a 350° oven for 50 to 60 minutes.

Serves 6.

—Louise and Hal Smith (Otis Campbell)

O'TIS A GREAT DAY!

Otis may not always begin the day in a cheery mood, but he usually ends up in good spirits.

Recipe from page 193 in *Aunt Bee's Mayberry Cookbook*
Rutledge Hill Press, Nashville, Tennessee

Mt. Pilot Pecan Pie

1 cup dark corn syrup
3 eggs, slightly beaten
⅛ teaspoon salt
1 teaspoon vanilla
1 cup sugar
2 tablespoons margarine, melted
1 cup pecans, chopped or halved
1 9-inch unbaked pie shell

In a large bowl combine all of the ingredients except the pie shell, adding the pecans last. Pour the mixture into the pastry shell. Bake in a 400° oven for 15 minutes. Reduce the heat to 350° and bake for 30 to 35 minutes. The pie is done when the outer edge of the filling is set and the center is slightly soft.

Serves 6 to 8.

LIFE NOT HARRIED

News is the only thing that travels at a fast clip around Floyd's Barbershop.

Recipe from page 196 in *Aunt Bee's Mayberry Cookbook*
Rutledge Hill Press, Nashville, Tennessee

Thelma Lou's Chocolate Cream Dessert

⅓ to ½ cup semisweet chocolate pieces
1 tablespoon water
3 eggs, separated
Heavy cream or whipped cream

In a double boiler over simmering water, melt the chocolate with the water, stirring until smooth. Remove from the heat and add the egg yolks one at a time, beating well after each addition. Beat the egg whites until stiff and fold gently into the chocolate mixture. Spoon lightly into sherbet glasses. Chill.

Serve with heavy cream or whipped cream, flavored with rum or vanilla.

Serves 4 to 6.
—*Betty Lynn (Thelma Lou)*

JUST HANGING AROUND

To say Barney's having a good time might be stretching things a bit.

Recipe from page 202 in *Aunt Bee's Mayberry Cookbook*
Rutledge Hill Press, Nashville, Tennessee

Newton Monroe's Pineapple Casserole

2 20-ounce cans chunk
    unsweetened pineapple,
    drained
¾ cup sugar
5 tablespoons all-purpose flour
1¾ cups grated cheddar
    cheese
¾ cup crushed Ritz crackers
½ cup butter, melted

Grease a large ovenproof bowl. Pour the pineapple into the prepared bowl. Combine the sugar and flour, and sprinkle over the pineapple. Sprinkle the grated cheese over the pineapple, then the cracker crumbs. Pour the butter over the top. Bake in a 350° oven for 30 minutes.

Serves 6 to 8.

BOY OH BOY OH BOY!
When it comes time to go fishing, Barney, Opie and Andy generally hook up together.

Recipe from page 209 in *Aunt Bee's Mayberry Cookbook*
Rutledge Hill Press, Nashville, Tennessee

Howie Pruitt's Supreme Chocolate Chip Cookies

2½ cups all-purpose flour
1 teaspoon baking soda
1 teaspoon salt
1 cup butter
¾ cup sugar
¾ cup brown sugar
1 teaspoon vanilla extract
2 eggs
1 12-ounce package chocolate chips
1 12-ounce package raisins
1 10-ounce package plain M&M
   candies

In a small bowl combine the flour, baking soda, and salt. Set aside. In a large bowl beat together the butter, sugar, brown sugar, and vanilla extract until creamy. Beat in the eggs. Gradually blend in the flour mixture. Stir in the chocolate and raisins. Drop the mixture by the tablespoon onto ungreased cookie sheets. Bake in a 375° oven for 9 to 11 minutes, until the edges are golden brown. Remove from the oven and place the M&M candies on top of the cookies while the cookies are still hot. Serve with cold milk.

Makes about 3 dozen.

—*Dennis Rush (Howie Pruitt)*

MIRACLE WORKERS

Opie and his pals need a miracle of their own to sell jars of Miracle Salve. (Cookie cook Dennis Rush is at far right.)

Recipe from page 212 in *Aunt Bee's Mayberry Cookbook*
Rutledge Hill Press, Nashville, Tennessee

Harvey's Little Big Orange Cookies

1 cup butter, softened
1 cup sugar
1 egg
1½ teaspoons orange extract
1 teaspoon grated orange peel
1½ cups sifted all-purpose flour
½ teaspoon salt

In a large bowl cream together the butter and sugar. Add the egg and the remaining ingredients. Drop by the spoonful onto an ungreased cookie sheet. Bake in a 375° oven for 10 minutes.

Makes 2 dozen.

—*Harvey Bullock (writer)*

WINGING IT

Harvey Bullock found the recipe for success when he wrote the memorable "Opie the Birdman" episode.

Recipe from page 214 in *Aunt Bee's Mayberry Cookbook*
Rutledge Hill Press, Nashville, Tennessee

Aunt Bee's Kerosene Cucumbers

Cucumbers
1 bunch dill
6 hot peppers
6 cloves garlic
6 slices onion
6 teaspoons whole spices
6 lumps alum
1 quart cider vinegar
2 quarts water
1 cup salt

Wash and dry enough cucumbers for six
sterilized 1-quart jars. In the bottom of each jar
place a portion of the dill, 1 hot pepper, 1 clove
of garlic, 1 slice of onion, 1 teaspoon of whole
spices, a small lump of alum, and cucumbers.
In a saucepan combine the vinegar, water, and
salt. Let the mixture come to a rolling boil,
then pour into the jars. Seal immediately.
   Makes 6 quarts.

PICKLED TINK

If you're in a bad pickle, just remember things were worse
with Aunt Bee's homemade pickles.
(But you'll have better luck with this recipe.)

Recipe from page 226 in *Aunt Bee's Mayberry Cookbook*
Rutledge Hill Press, Nashville, Tennessee

Cousin Leda's Banana Chutney

6 bananas
1 cup minced onion
1 cup raisins
1 cup minced tart apples
1 cup apple cider vinegar
2 cups sugar
1 tablespoon salt
1 teaspoon ground ginger
1 teaspoon nutmeg
¼ cup cayenne pepper
⅓ cup lemon juice
3 cloves garlic, minced

Peel and mash the bananas. In a large casserole dish combine all of the ingredients. Bake in a 350° oven for about 2 hours, stirring occasionally.

When thickened, ladle into sterilized jars and seal.

Makes about 2 pints.

—*Deane Ward and Everett Greenbaum (writer)*

HAVING A BALL

Barney, Gomer and Andy wish you were here (and they weren't)
as they search for clues in the haunted house.

Recipe from page 229 in *Aunt Bee's Mayberry Cookbook*
Rutledge Hill Press, Nashville, Tennessee